Who Is Shohei Ohtani?

Who Is
Shohei Ohtani?

by James Buckley Jr.

illustrated by Gregory Copeland

Penguin Workshop

To the Santa Barbara Foresters,
for bringing me 10 championship rings—JB

PENGUIN WORKSHOP
An imprint of Penguin Random House LLC
1745 Broadway, New York, New York 10019

First published in the United States of America by Penguin Workshop,
an imprint of Penguin Random House LLC, 2025

PENGUIN is a registered trademark and PENGUIN WORKSHOP is a trademark
of Penguin Books Ltd. WHO HQ & Design is a registered trademark
of Penguin Random House LLC.

Visit us online at penguinrandomhouse.com.

Library of Congress Cataloging-in-Publication Data is available.

Printed in the United States of America

ISBN 9780593888285 (paperback)   10 9 8 7 6 5 4   CJKW
ISBN 9780593888292 (library binding)   10 9 8 7 6 5 4 3 2 1 CJKW

The authorized representative in the EU for product safety and compliance is
Penguin Random House Ireland, Morrison Chambers, 32 Nassau Street,
Dublin D02 YH68, Ireland, https://eu-contact.penguin.ie.

Contents

Who Is Shohei Ohtani?

On July 27, 2023, the Los Angeles Angels' starting pitcher threw a great game. He allowed only one hit and no runs in nine innings. He also struck out eight Detroit Tigers, and his team won, 6–0. It was one of the best games he had thrown since joining the team.

It was also the first game of a doubleheader. In the second game, the Angels' designated hitter (DH) had two home runs and three runs batted in (RBI). The Angels won that game 11–4.

But the big news of the day was that the pitcher and the DH were the *same player*—the very talented Shohei Ohtani (say: SHOW-hay oh-TAHN-ee). It was the first time in baseball history that a player pitched a complete-game shutout in one game, then hit two homers in the second game.

Breaking barriers in baseball was nothing new for Shohei.

Not only was he one of the best hitters in the sport, he was also a dominant pitcher. Few players had ever been both of those things, and none of them had achieved as much as Shohei. He also was a terrific base stealer! Wherever Shohei played, fans, teammates, and opponents were amazed at how he could be so good at so many different skills.

Even as he became one of the most famous athletes on the planet, he remained humble, focused, and dedicated. He cared only about baseball and his family, letting his play do the talking for him.

When he moved to the Los Angeles Dodgers of Major League Baseball (MLB) for the 2024 season, his star grew even brighter. Sports has never seen an athlete like Shohei who can do it all. Let's find out how he got to the top of the baseball world.

CHAPTER 1
The Future Superstar

Shohei Ohtani was born on July 5, 1994, in the farming town of Mizusawa, Japan (today, the town is called Oshu). It is about three hundred miles north of the capital, Tokyo. Shohei was born into a sports-loving family. His father, Toru, played baseball for a team at the machine parts company where he worked. His mother, Kayoko, had been a top badminton player when she was younger. Shohei's older brother, Ryuta, loved baseball, while his older sister, Yuka, played volleyball.

Shohei soon picked baseball as his favorite sport.

"I watched baseball players and they looked so cool," he said. "I was always anxiously waiting for the weekend so I could play."

Toru gave Shohei his first baseball glove, a red-and-black Spalding, when Shohei was five or six years old. When Ryuta was growing up, Toru had felt bad that he did not spend enough time with him. So when Shohei was young, Toru took a new job that allowed him enough free time to teach Shohei to play baseball—how to hit, field, and pitch. Shohei became a *yakyu shonen*—a kid who does nothing but play and think about baseball. When Shohei was eight, he joined his first baseball team. But he was not sure how well he would do. "I grew up in the countryside of Japan, where there were few baseball teams, where most of the teams had never been to big tournaments," he remembered. "I was sure many players outshined me in talent."

Also, his new league did not allow multicolored gloves. Shohei loved the glove his father had given him, so he got a marker and colored the red areas black!

Toru also gave Shohei a notebook. He would write notes about how Shohei did after every game and practice. Shohei would read the notes, and then add his own. Toru taught Shohei to focus on communicating with his teammates and to always hustle on the field.

Shohei's life was not all baseball. He sometimes played badminton with his mom, and in the winter there was often enough snow to go sledding. He also loved taking swimming lessons. And he enjoyed spending time with the family dog, a golden retriever named Ace.

Baseball soon became number one, though. He played on youth teams for several years, always working on improving his skills. He was both a hitter who played outfield and a pitcher, which is not unusual on younger teams.

By middle school, Shohei says, he was "way larger than average." Toru helped coach Shohei's junior high team, the Ichinoseki Little Seniors.

In one game Shohei pitched, he struck out seventeen of eighteen batters. Shohei moved on to Hanamaki Higashi High School for baseball . . . and more writing! The coach there asked the team to write down their goals as players. Shohei still has the paper he wrote. He divided his goals into eight main areas, including fitness, mental attitude, hitting, and pitching.

"I think it helps to put it in writing," he said later of his goals chart. "Writing and posting notes where you can see them is a simple act, but I think it's effective. As you continue what you've written, the things you need to do will eventually become second nature."

Hanamaki was a boarding school, so Shohei lived on campus most of the year. His high school coach, Hiroshi Sasaki, gave the players jobs in the dorms. Pitchers like Shohei always cleaned the bathrooms.

Shohei also began watching videos of

professional stars in the Nippon Professional Baseball league in Japan and MLB in the United States and Canada. He looked for tips on hitting and pitching. Because Shohei hit left-handed, he watched MLB star outfielder Ken Griffey Jr. The very tall left-handed pitcher Randy Johnson became a model for Shohei, too. He also loved watching Hideki Matsui, a strong hitter who had gone from Japan to the US Major Leagues.

"Even as a child, it was clear to me that MLB was the place for top-tier baseball," said Shohei.

Shohei was soon an all-around star in high school baseball, which is a much bigger sport in Japan than in the United States. The annual high school tournament, called the Koshien, is one of Japan's biggest sports events. In 2012, Shohei pitched in the Koshien and threw a fastball at almost a hundred miles per hour! It shocked fans and put him on the national baseball map. By the time he graduated, he stood six feet, four inches tall and weighed more than two hundred pounds. Every Japanese pro team wanted to choose him in the Nippon Professional Baseball (NPB) draft. Shohei had other ideas.

"I agonized over the decision," he announced before the draft in 2013. "But I have decided to play in America. It's been my dream to play in the majors since I started school. I want to play over there as early as possible. I will learn the hard way. I understand the risks. It's not about the money. It's about following my dream."

Baseball in Japan

Baseball has been played in Japan since the 1870s, when an American professor named Horace Wilson first showed his Japanese students how to play. The game quickly grew in popularity, and is now the country's favorite sport to play and to watch.

After a team of MLB All-Stars toured Japan in 1934, baseball became big enough to start a professional league two years later. Today, it's called Nippon Professional Baseball. (*Nippon* is the name of the nation in the Japanese language.) NPB includes the Central League and the Pacific League. Twelve teams play 143 games each per NPB season.

The league champions meet in the Japan Series to determine an overall winner.

Thousands of young people play baseball in Japan, from youth leagues to high schools. The annual Koshien high school tournament is watched by millions, and teams from Japan have won eleven Little League World Series. Japan's national team has won the World Baseball Classic (WBC) three out of five times, as well as winning two Olympic baseball tournaments.

CHAPTER 2
A Hero in Japan

Even though Shohei said he wanted to play in the United States for MLB, Japan's Nippon-Ham Fighters picked him first overall in the draft anyway. They wanted to convince him not to leave Japan. Fighters general manager Masao Yamada made a presentation for Shohei and his parents called "The Path to Realizing Shohei Ohtani's Dream." Yamada pointed out that Shohei would have to start in the lower-level minor leagues in the United States. In Japan, top high school players can go right to the top, the NPB. Plus, Yamada said, if Shohei joined the Fighters, he could be a *nito-ryu* (two-way player). No one else, even the teams in MLB, had said he could both pitch and hit for them. While Shohei could do both in high school, he would have had to specialize in pitching or hitting at the pro level.

During one visit to the Ohtani home, several Fighters officials helped their case by giving special attention to the family dog, Ace. Shohei noticed. And then he listened carefully to the Fighters presentations.

Finally, Shohei surprised everyone by choosing to stay in Japan and join the Fighters. It meant he would get a lower salary than he might from MLB, but he would get to both pitch and hit.

He did get a bonus of more than $1 million, plus signed up lots of sponsorships. He also enjoyed free ham, because that's what the company that owns the Fighters produced.

"I had hoped to go directly to the US after high school," he said later. "All the other Japanese teams only wanted me as a pitcher. There were offers from US teams, but they also saw me only as a pitcher. The Fighters were the only team to propose such an idea. I thought it through and made my choice."

He was going to try something that no one in Japan had done. Only a very few MLB players had ever tried it, either. If Shohei could succeed at both, he would be one of a kind.

Even with all the attention he had received in high school, Shohei was surprised by how much the media followed him once he turned pro and joined the Fighters. Hundreds of reporters attended every practice and every game, watching him do everything from the moment he left the team dorm. Still, he tried to focus on the game.

Shohei got two hits in his first game. He made his first appearance on the pitcher's mound a few weeks later. He struggled a bit getting used to pro play, but had a pretty good season. Still, he was so famous that fans voted Shohei into the All-Star Game as a pitcher and as an outfielder!

In 2014, Shohei became the first player in Japan to reach double digits in both wins as a pitcher and home runs as a hitter. He was also the first player in *any* major league to do that since 1918, when Babe Ruth accomplished it for MLB's Boston Red Sox. Ruth went on to be one of baseball's all-time great sluggers, and Shohei was soon compared to him.

Before the 2016 season, Shohei worked out in Japan with former Fighters superstar and MLB pitcher Yu Darvish. He focused on flexibility and worked with weights. He also changed his diet, cutting out sugar and switching to healthier brown rice. Shohei knew that talent would only take him so far. He had to work just as hard away from the field.

Throughout his time with the Fighters, Shohei lived in a team dorm during the season. It's not unusual for NPB first-year players to do this, but Shohei kept it up even as he got older. In a team dorm, the players stay together, watched over by coaches. They actually have to get permission before they leave the dorm to do anything. When he was not playing, Shohei said that he liked reading about baseball and watching sports movies. His favorites included *Rudy* and *Remember the Titans*.

In 2016, Shohei had his best season yet.

He led the Japan League in earned run average (1.86), which is the average number of runs that a pitcher allows the other team to score in nine innings. He also threw 174 strikeouts in only 140 innings and won the Home Run Derby at the All-Star Game. He and the Fighters won the Japan Series, too, giving them their first NPB championship since 2006. Following the season, Shohei was the Pacific League Most Valuable Player (MVP), and was named to the league's Best Nine as both a pitcher and as the designated hitter. No other Japanese player had ever done that.

After five seasons with the Fighters, Shohei began to remember his childhood dream. "I've always had a desire to play in [Major League Baseball]," he said. "I don't know exactly when that's going to be. But when I feel ready to go, I'll go." In 2017, he was ready.

The Fighters celebrate their win

CHAPTER 3
Coming to America

When a player leaves Japan to play in America, MLB teams have to make a financial offer to the player's Japanese team. They also have to give the player a contract, usually for a lot of money. Then the player and his NPB team choose the best deal. Several MLB teams made offers for Shohei—as well as presentations about their ball clubs.

Some teams even had their star players reach out to Shohei to try to convince him. Shohei had a video call with Mike Trout, the superstar outfielder for the Los Angeles Angels.

"He basically explained to me how great the Angels were, how they have a great clubhouse, and how he would enjoy having me here. And

I took those words to heart," Shohei said. The Angels also offered him a bonus of $2.3 million and agreed to pay the Fighters $20 million.

On November 11, 2017, Shohei announced that he had signed to play with the Angels.

Shohei went to spring training with the Angels in Arizona. His parents flew over to see his first exhibition games. On March 29, 2018, he played in his first official Angels game and got a hit in his first at-bat. In each of the next three games, he hit home runs. He also showed off another talent—speed. He soon became one of the fastest players in the American League.

In his second start as a pitcher, he threw seven innings while allowing only one hit and no runs.

Shohei received a lot of love from the people who cheered for the Angels. "The fans made me feel very welcomed. That's one of the reasons why I was able to focus on my performance. I consider myself very lucky and thankful for my situation."

While he was comfortable on the field, Shohei faced challenges off it. He had moved to a new country, and he didn't speak much English. He also had to meet new teammates and coaches. And he wanted to find places to get his favorite Japanese food. He had help, though. Ippei (say: IH-pay) Mizuhara came to the United States with Shohei from the Fighters. He was Shohei's interpreter and soon became his best friend. Ippei had grown up in the United States, so he knew the culture and he understood American baseball.

Shohei's Angels teammates were very welcoming. They tried to teach him both English and Spanish, and they helped him when the team traveled to different cities to play. When he was at home, he was never far from the clubhouse. Shohei lived in an apartment building across the parking lot from Angel Stadium!

That didn't stop them from teasing him just like they did other rookies. After Shohei hit his first home run, the fans at Angel Stadium cheered for him. But when Shohei came back to the dugout after touching home plate, his teammates just turned their backs. He tried to high-five them, but they didn't want to. Shohei was not sure what was going on. After a moment, though, the entire team surrounded him and patted him on the back and congratulated him. It turned out Shohei was the victim of a famous big-league prank—pretending to ignore a player's big moment.

After hitting four homers and reaching 101.1 miles per hour with a fastball while winning two of his four starts as a pitcher, Shohei was named the American League (AL) Rookie of the Month for April 2018.

In the early summer, he suffered a minor elbow injury and could only pitch once more after June.

However, he pitched enough to match the great Babe Ruth again: Shohei joined Ruth as the only other player to pitch at least 50 innings and hit 15 or more homers in a season. In September, Shohei got the bad news that he would need surgery on his pitching elbow. He ended the season with 22 homers, 61 runs batted in, and a .285 batting average. In November, he was named the AL Rookie of the Year.

His next stop was a hospital to have surgery. Shohei would not be able to pitch again until 2020.

CHAPTER 4
Better Than Babe?

The next two MLB seasons were very difficult for Shohei. He wanted to pitch, but he had to let his arm heal. He was still able to help the Angels as a hitter, and had a good season in 2019. He hoped to pitch in 2020, but then the COVID-19 pandemic hit in March. The MLB season didn't start until late July. Shohei's first game back on the mound as a pitcher went very badly. He allowed five hits and three runs . . . and didn't get any batters out. The team decided to wait until 2021 to have him pitch again regularly.

Shohei later said that the year after his surgery "was also a struggle. I didn't feel that I was recovering how I should. I started to doubt.

I honestly considered dropping the two-way path."

Then came the 2021 season. During spring training, Shohei was called into Angels manager Joe Maddon's office. "I was told there would be no rules for me, and they'd play me without any restrictions that season," said Shohei. To Shohei, that meant that the Angels were telling him this was his last chance. He had to make it as a two-way player (as both a pitcher and a hitter) that season or they wouldn't let him try in the future.

It turned out that was *not* what Maddon meant. Instead, the Angels thought they were giving him freedom and trust to play the way he wanted to. Either way, it worked. Shohei had his best overall season yet. The Angels let Shohei tell them when he needed rest and when he was ready to play. And he was ready a lot—he played 155 games, his most in a season yet.

In one game, Shohei threw a pitch 100 miles per hour, then hit a homer that flew at 115 miles per hour! In June, he hit a home run that traveled 470 feet, still among the longest he had ever hit.

In July, he was the first player ever chosen for two positions in the MLB All-Star Game. He also took part in the Home Run Derby. He didn't win, but his 513-foot longball was the longest of the contest. The next night, he was the starting pitcher *and* the DH for the American League team.

By the end of the season, Shohei was fully back to being the complete player he wanted to be.

Shohei hit a career-high 46 homers and had 100 RBI, along with 26 stolen bases. He also won nine games as a pitcher and averaged more than 10 strikeouts per nine innings. He got all 30 first-place votes and was named the AL Most Valuable Player. The only negative of his season was that the Angels, even with Shohei and Trout, won only 77 of 162 games.

As good as he was in 2021, Shohei was even better in 2022. He won 15 games as a pitcher and lowered his earned run average (ERA) to 2.33.

He led all pitchers by averaging 11.9 strikeouts per nine innings. He had 34 homers along with 95 RBI and made the All-Star team again. He finished second to Aaron Judge of the New York Yankees in the MVP voting, but the Angels had a losing record again.

CHAPTER 5
A World Championship
and a New Team

Before his 2023 season with the Angels, Shohei took the field for another team: Japan. Shohei joined the best players from his country in the World Baseball Classic (WBC). The international tournament is held every three years for the world's best baseball nations.

Japan won its first four games easily. Then it defeated Italy and Mexico in the playoffs to reach the championship game. Their opponent would be the United States team, filled with MLB players Shohei knew—including his Angels teammate, Mike Trout.

LoanDepot Park in Miami was packed for the championship game. More than five million more people watched on TV in the United States. And 29 million people watched in Japan, even though the game started there at eight in the morning!

The two teams marched into the stadium. Shohei led the way for Japan, carrying his country's flag. He had pitched five days earlier against Italy, then had two hits and scored two runs in a semifinal win over Mexico. Before the final, he told his manager that he would be able to pitch late in this big game if needed. With two homers in the first four innings, Japan took a 3–1 lead. Then the US team added a run in the eighth inning.

Japan led 3–2 in the bottom of the ninth. As fans rose to their feet cheering, Shohei made his way to the mound. He had not pitched at the end of a game since 2016, but now his country needed him. He walked the first batter, but then got a double play. That brought Trout to the plate. Trout was a three-time AL MVP and one of the best players in baseball.

It was an epic battle, with fans of both teams screaming in delight.

Shohei fired fastballs and curveballs. Trout swung at some and let others go by. The noise only increased as the count reached 3 and 2.

"I sensed that the game was heading to a close with me striking Mike out," Shohei said later. He was right. Trout swung and missed. Japan had won the WBC title. Shohei shouted and threw his cap and glove as his teammates ran out to jump and dance on the field.

For winning two games as a pitcher and saving another, plus hitting .435 with eight RBI, Shohei was named the WBC MVP.

The next time Shohei saw Trout, they were both Los Angeles Angels again. By the middle of the 2023 season, Shohei was continuing to excel. He was at the top of many hitting stats and was pitching as well as ever. But in September, he needed another surgery on his pitching elbow. He had to stop pitching for 2023 and would not be able to pitch at all in 2024, just as he had missed 2019. He was able to finish the 2023 season as a hitter and led the AL with 44 homers and 325 total bases. As a pitcher, he won 10 games with a 3.14 ERA. For the second time, Shohei got all the first-place votes and was the AL MVP. That made him the first player to win two MVP awards while getting all the first-place votes.

He got the news about that 2023 award on a

video call, during which fans got to see Shohei's new dog, Decoy, for the first time! Later, he put out a statement that thanked his family, his fans, his coaches, and the country of Japan, along with his Angels teammates. But by the time of that video call, he was not an Angel anymore.

After the 2023 season, his contract with the Angels was over. Shohei was free to sign with any team. Of course, many teams made him offers. Who wouldn't want the best overall player in baseball? Shohei had another big decision to make. He was already making more money than any other player. One report said that with money from sponsors and from the Angels, he had made more than $65 million in 2023.

In December, he used some of that money to buy sixty thousand baseball gloves to donate to schools in Japan. "This is just the beginning," he said about his gift. Later that month, he gave his new team a really big gift, too.

After listening to all the offers, Shohei made his choice. On December 11, 2023, he signed a ten-year contract worth $700 million to play for the Los Angeles Dodgers. It was the biggest deal in baseball history. But Shohei did something very unusual. He asked the Dodgers to only pay him $2 million per year for ten seasons. They could pay him the rest of the money after that. Shohei's generosity meant that the Dodgers would have more money available to sign other players. He wanted to win a World Series so much that he would take far less money than he was owed.

Not long after the event at Dodger Stadium, Shohei announced that he got married in the offseason. His wife is Mamiko Tanaka, a former pro basketball player in Japan.

With Shohei on the team, the Dodgers

became one of the hottest tickets in baseball. His first regular-season game with them was played in South Korea (MLB often starts the season in other countries to help promote the sport). Mamiko was able to see him play in person for the first time.

But after that game, Shohei received some shocking news. Ippei Mizuhara, his friend and interpreter, had gotten in trouble for gambling on sports, though not on baseball. He said that Shohei had helped him pay back his gambling losses. Shohei said this was not true. Shohei was shocked and met with Ippei. Soon, Ippei told the truth. He had stolen more than $16 million from Shohei to pay for his gambling. Shohei was very hurt that a person he trusted so much had stolen from him and lied about it. But he tried hard not to let his problems off the field hurt his performance on it.

On April 21, Shohei hit his 176th homer in MLB. That was the most ever by a player from Japan. Fans and writers continued to compare him to Babe Ruth. In fact, through each player's first 725 games, they each had exactly 176 home runs! Plus, they had almost exactly the same pitching record. By the midseason of 2024, Shohei was leading the National League in home runs, total bases, and slugging percentage. He even had a big home run in the 2024 MLB All-Star Game, too. Shohei's homers kept flying out of ballparks, some going places no one had ever seen. "Good gracious," said Dodgers pitcher Clayton Kershaw after watching Shohei's 30th homer. "I don't think I've seen a ball go that far before."

On August 23, he stole his 40th base of the season and hit his 40th home run, which put him in the "40-40 club"—something only five other players had done in Major League

Baseball to that point. The homer was also a walk-off grand slam that won the game for the Dodgers. "[It was] one of my top memorable moments," he said. "And I hope that I can do more and have more memorable moments."

He didn't have to wait long. A few days later, fans at Dodger Stadium lined up for hours to get a bobblehead figurine of Shohei and his dog, Decoy. Before the game, Decoy "threw" the ceremonial first pitch by carrying a baseball from the mound to Shohei waiting at home plate!

Then on September 19, 2024, Shohei stunned the baseball world. While leading the Dodgers to a 20–4 win over the Miami Marlins, Shohei had six hits, three of them homers. He drove in 10 runs and stole two bases. No one had ever done all that in one game. Some experts called it the greatest performance by a batter in history. His homers and steals that day also made him the only member of the 50-50 club, with 51 homers and 51 steals at that point in the season.

The Dodgers finished with the best record in MLB. They beat the San Diego Padres and the New York Mets. In the playoffs, Shohei kept making an impact. At one point, he had 17 hits in 20 at-bats with teammates on base.

In the World Series, the Dodgers faced the New York Yankees and their own famous slugger, Aaron Judge. In game 2, Shohei hurt his shoulder on a slide. He kept hitting, but he didn't have the same power. Still, the Dodgers won in five games, and Shohei's World Series dream came true!

At the victory parade, he waved from atop a bus with Decoy and Mamiko. At Dodger Stadium, he surprised fans by speaking in English. "This is such a special moment for me. I'm so honored to be here and be part of this team. Congratulations, Los Angeles. Thank you, guys!"

Shohei ended the 2024 season with 54 home

runs and 59 stolen bases. He led the NL with 130 RBI and a .646 slugging percentage. He led all of MLB with 411 total bases and 134 runs scored—plus, of course, that World Series championship! In November 2024, Shohei won his third MVP award. He was the first DH to be named MVP and only the second player to win an MVP in both the AL and NL.

He'll return to the mound for the 2025 Dodgers season, when the team's first game was scheduled to be in Japan.

Hideki Kuriyama, Shohei's former Fighters manager, says it best: "I'm convinced that he's going to blow us away even more in the future."

Timeline of Shohei Ohtani's Life

1994	Born on July 5 in present-day Oshu, Iwate, Japan
1999	Receives his first baseball glove from his father
2002	Joins first organized baseball team at age eight
2012	Stars for his high-school team in Koshien tournament
2013	Drafted first overall by Nippon-Ham Fighters
2016	Named Pacific League MVP after leading Fighters to Japan Series championship
2018	Joins Los Angeles Angels; named American League Rookie of the Year
	Has operation on arm; will not pitch again until 2020
2021	First player chosen as MLB All-Star as both pitcher and hitter
	Wins AL Most Valuable Player award
2022	Finishes second in AL MVP voting
2023	Leads Japan to World Baseball Classic title
	Wins second AL MVP award
	Has second arm operation, and will not pitch in 2024
	Signs biggest contract in MLB history with Los Angeles Dodgers
2024	Marries Mamiko Tanaka
	Hits three-run home run in MLB All-Star Game

Timeline of the World

1997 — The Mars Pathfinder mission lands the Sojourner rover on the surface of Mars

2002 — The new country of East Timor, formerly part of Indonesia, becomes the 191st member of the United Nations

2007 — Apple introduces the iPhone

2010 — The Burj Khalifa opens in Dubai, the tallest building in the world at 163 stories

2011 — After 135 missions since 1981, the US space shuttle program ends

2016 — Great Britain votes to leave the European Union, a process called "Brexit"

2019 — The coronavirus disease COVID-19 first emerges and spreads around the world in a global pandemic that will kill more than two million people by 2022

2021 — Ingenuity, a robot helicopter on Mars, becomes the first humanmade craft to fly on another planet

2022 — Russia invades the neighboring country of Ukraine

2023 — Scientists announce that 2023 was the warmest year in recorded history

2024 — Breakdancers compete at the Olympics for the first time

Bibliography

*Books for young readers

*Downs, Kieran. ***Shohei Ohtani***. Minnetonka, MN: Bellwether, 2023.

*Fishman, Jon M. ***Shohei Ohtani***. Minneapolis: Lerner, 2022.

Hernandez, Dylan. "Early On, He Redefined What Was Possible in the Sport." ***Los Angeles Times***, September 29, 2017.

Paris, Jay. ***Shohei Ohtani: The Amazing Story of Baseball's Two-Way Japanese Superstar***. New York: Sports Publishing, 2018.

Tokikawa, Toru, dir. ***Shohei Ohtani: Beyond the Dream***. ESPN Films, 2023.

Verducci, Tom. "The Icon Among Us." ***Sports Illustrated***, April 2024.

Zwelling, Arden. "The Next Babe Ruth: How Shohei Ohtani Became Baseball's Most Dominant Two-Way Player in a Century." ***Sportsnet***, 2017.

YOUR HEADQUARTERS FOR HISTORY

Activities, Mad Libs, and sidesplitting jokes!
Discover the Who HQ books beyond the biographies